LOVE

Chronicles of Seemorgh & The Three Warriors

by Mariam Touzie

About Birth (book 1)

"I thoroughly enjoyed it. Great work! Congratulations! You make a very important point about our epic stories and their relevance to our daily life. That is indeed the case if one taps into the true meaning of the stories. Symbolism plays an important role here. This is what I got out of the story:

Saum is at the height of power and popularity. He has a beautiful wife. He is strong, courageous, loyal, handsome In short, he is everything a man wishes to be! The king, the court, the power, are all the symbols of the best this world has to offer. But Saum has only excelled in the worldly dimensions. He does not have foresight about the world beyond, and meaning of the events happening to him. He can only comprehend and accept the conventional wisdom (Aghl) God throws an unconventional gift at him. This gift is something he does not recognize! Because it is very different than his expectation. The boy (Zahl) is old looking, symbolizing divine wisdom before it's time! as he is only a baby. Saum is entangled in his ego, so he does not value the gift. So he rejects it in outrage. God, takes the gift back and preserves him, until Saum becomes ready, he gets the needed signals. Finally, he will seek the gift and endures much hardship to regain what he had all along at some point. When he finally get it, appreciation comes with understanding. Later Zahl produces Rostam, the beloved hero which combines the earthly and divine powers. So the moral of the story is that we have all these potentials within us. and sometimes out of nowhere, they surface, but we reject the precious opportunity out of ignorance and conformity. In fact "The things in our lives which make a difference are indeed different!"

— *Dr. Sadri Khalessi, Stanford University , CA.,*

to my brothers and their loving wives

I wish to extend my gratitude to my friends who supported and advised me, without their help I would not be able to complete this book. Nilou Safavieh for the design and Maryam Pirnazar for the edit.

ISBN-13: 978-0-9855399-1-7

Published by Zayandeh Publications, New York City

Printed in United Stats of America

ZAYANDEH PUBLICATIONS

Book 2

LOVE

Chronicles of Seemorgh & The Three Warriors

Inspired by:
The Book of Kings epic poem by *Ferdowsi Toosi*

by Mariam Touzie

Love is the affair of Zal and Roudabeh, Princess of Kabol.

Zal, son of Saum the great warrior, was born thousands of years ago in Zabolestan, in the Iranian heartland. His mother died at childbirth and his father disowned him because of his head of white hair and, his huge strong body that could belong to a two year old. Years later Saum retraces his steps and reclaims his abandoned son. In the intervening years Zal was discovered and raised by Seemorgh, the legendary bird.

Roudabeh was the only child of the King of Kabol, Mehrab, whose great, great, great grandfather was Zahhak! Zahhak was the greedy son of a benevolent landowner who was kissed by the devil personified as a cook of sumptuous food. From the spots where he was kissed two deadly snakes grew on Zahhak's shoulders. The snakes had to be fed the brains of two young men every day.

The story may be old and fantastic, but it represents our most familiar feeling: Love. The light that Ferdowsi sheds on Zal's path of life is so strong that it peels off all layers of illusion and allows love to shine forth.

Characters in order of appearance

Saum: Greatest among the warriors of the kingdom

Zal: Son of Saum

A friend of Mehrab, King of Kabol

Mehrab: King of Kabol

Ceendokht: Queen of Kabol

Roudabeh: Daughter of Mehrab & Ceendokht

Seemorgh: A mythological bird in ancient Iran

Prince Nozar: Son of King Manoochehr

King Manoochehr: King of all Iran

Kaveh the Smitten: The man who finally defeated and banished Zahhak

Zahhak: Mehrab's great, great, great, grandfather and son of a benevolent land-owner, whose greed had no boundaries. He was kissed on his shoulders by the impersonation of the devil through many tricks. Two snakes grew on the spots at the moment he was kissed. He lived his life solely to provide for the two always-hungry snakes on his shoulders, until Kaveh the Iranian ironsmith stopped him forever with help from his sons and friends.

Zal begins his new life with Saum the warrior, his newly-found father.

Saum takes his son to see the land, and show him the living beings in the place that Zal calls home now.

Saum employs the most skillful warriors to teach Zal the use of a spear and bow and arrow, as well as swordsmanship and all styles of hand-to-hand combat. Then he invites brilliant scientists and master poets to live with them and teach Zal. Saum arranges all this before leaving for his next mission by the Caspian Sea.

The warrior advises Zal: "Learn all that your teachers teach you, then travel to see the world with your own eyes. Make friends, and be generous with your friends with both affection and riches."

Zal is an eager student. He goes through his learning stages with great speed and flying colors. Then he sets off to travel with the friends he has made in his learning life.

Mehrab, King of Kabol, hears that Zal is visiting his land. He is most curious about Zal — the child who was raised by Seemorgh and trained by the best masters to be a man. So he rides to the hunting ground with a large entourage and precious gifts to meet Zal.

Zal is pleased. He invites Mehrab to his camp. The two men engage in many conversations lasting all day long.

"Please come to the castle and have dinner with us tonight," suggests Mehrab.

"I am most grateful for your invitation but I am not able to accept," Zal responds – and then he adds: "I would be glad to ride home with you."

The two men say their warm good-byes at sunset by Mehrab's castle. Roudabeh steals glances at Zal and Ceendokht comes forward in wonder. Her husband has a lot to say about his meeting with Zal.

A close companion of Mehrab approaches Zal on the way back to his camp and says: "If you think Mehrab is an impressive man you should meet his daughter and his wife!"

"Why?" asks Zal.

"They are the embodiment of beauty on earth."

"That is wonderful, dear Sir."

"The Queen trained her daughter to have a great mind as well."

"Very nice."

"Please listen to me."

"I do."

"Then think of her tonight!"

"Why should I?"

"Because you are Zal, the fantastic child of the greatest warrior, and she is a divine daughter of a King," says the man before leaving Zal. The man leaves, but Zal is perturbed all night long!

The next day he decides to remain impervious to all the man had said to him the night before.

Roudabeh cries all night. When her friends come around and ask her the reason, she says:

"I am in love!"

"Oh! Who is the lucky Prince?" Asks one of the friends.

"What's his name?' Wonders another.

"Zal!"

"Ah.... Wow...!" They are all surprised: "Son of the famous warrior Saum?"

Another friend questions Roudabeh with great concern, adding: "Zal was born with all white hair like an old man and he speaks the language of birds!"

Roudabeh is now offended! She exclaims with frustration: "He was raised by Seemorgh, but you should have heard my father last night if you want to know how Zal speaks." Then she continues: "I saw his gorgeous white hair last night. That is a big part of his charm."

"You are in love!" All of her friends agree.

"But he does not even know me," Roudabeh cries.

"We should help arrange a secret meeting," one of the friends suggests.

Zal agrees!

Soon enough, friends of Roudabeh appear near the camp of Zal and casually get close to Zal's confidants. They arrange the secret meeting, and Zal agrees to meet Roudabeh at her quarters that same night.

Zal emerges from the forest near Mehrab's castle where Roudabeh's quarters are located. He slips through the window after climbing up the high wall and says: "I arrive like a burglar my lady, please forgive me!"

Roudabeh helps him inside the room, saying nothing. Her stunning beauty captures Zal.

Their faces glow while looking at one another, something that neither of them had imagined before.

Soon they begin to talk in the manner of two old friends, sincerely and lovingly. They tell each other about their childhood.

The most interesting story for Roudabeh is the one when Zal insisted on learning to walk as Seemorgh taught her own young to fly.

The night goes by fast!

At dawn neither one of them can tell at which exact moment they fell in love – only that the feeling was to remain with them for a lifetime.

They would marry right away if they could! But they agree to strive toward their goal gently and quietly. They are perfectly aware of the horrible history that would come to play a part in their wonderful marriage plans.

"I'll dispatch a messenger to my father" Zal promises.

"I will wait," Roudabeh responds joyously.

Zal conveys a letter to Saum as soon as he returns to his camp.

Faraway, by the northern mountains near the Caspian Sea, Saum opens his son's letter. He rejoices! Then worries attack him: "What if Roudabeh turns out to be like her great, great, great grandfather?" He has deep concerns. "What if their children become like Zahhak?" he worries.

The warrior realizes that he needs insight!

He orders his son's messenger to eat and rest until it is time to relay the response. Then he gathers together astrologers and other trusted friends who practice the arts of divination. He tells them about the romance of Zal and Roudabeh, saying: "My dear friends, cast your horoscopes, consult planets, search for all omens, and use every splendid tool you know to give me an insight into this matter."

At the appointed hour all the warrior's friends arrive with great news.

"This is a fruitful affair!" announces the first wiseman.

"There will be child, a boy, who will be stronger than you and Zal put together," says a lady sage.

"He will be handsome, charming, and placid as a house cat, but braver than ten lions put together," the soothsayer adds.

"He will be the only warrior to wipe the land clean of all demons!"

"This child will look like you in appearance, but taller!"

"Indomitable!"

One by one they brighten the warrior's heart. Saum's thoughts are now clearer. He notes that for generations now no one from that family has turned out like Zahhak.

"Father approves!" Zal writes to Roudabeh.
Then he carefully searches and finds a well-trusted
woman to carry his letter directly to Roudabeh.

'What mischief are you up to here? Why were you coming out of my daughter's room?" demands Ceendokht to know as soon as she spots Zal's messenger in her castle.

"Nothing!" responds the speechless messenger who is caught by the queen. Then she collects her thoughts and comes up with an excuse: "I was fulfilling the lady's order. A specialty fabric...."

Ceendokht does not let her finish. She is not convinced and sends the woman to the dungeon until she reveals her secret. But the woman accepts her horrible fortune and keeps her lips sealed!

"Mother!" calls the devastated Roudabeh. She begs her mother to forgive the woman. "Sweet mother, please release this innocent woman and I will tell you everything."

She shows her mother the two crowns that she intended to send to Zal as the symbol of their commitment.

Mehrab is horrified when he hears! In the quiet of the
night, when Ceendokht speaks of Zal romancing
their daughter, Mehrab can only think of the horror
of his world coming to an end. He says indignantly:
"We are ruined."

He too, just like Saum the warrior when he first
hears of this love story, thinks of Zahhak and the
evil that was unleashed for years. His great, great,
great, grandfather! He knows well that the king
of Iran has no tolerance for such a marriage. He
protests: "I must wage war first!"

"Give me the keys to your finest treasures,"
Ceendokht demands of her husband. "I will collect
the grandest peace offering and visit Saum the
warrior in person," she adds.

"If you believe you can stop a war this way then
have it all," Mehrab responds, handing her the keys.

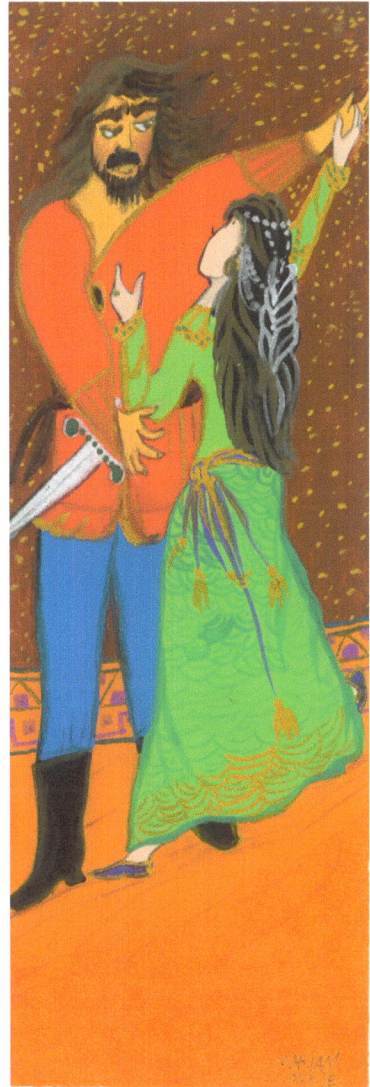

King Manoochehr sends his son Prince Nozar to the camp of Saum the warrior. "Father is confident that you have safeguarded this area of the north. Perhaps it is a good time to come back home," says the Prince at dinner. Saum is glad to go home and looks forward to speaking with the King about Zal and his future.

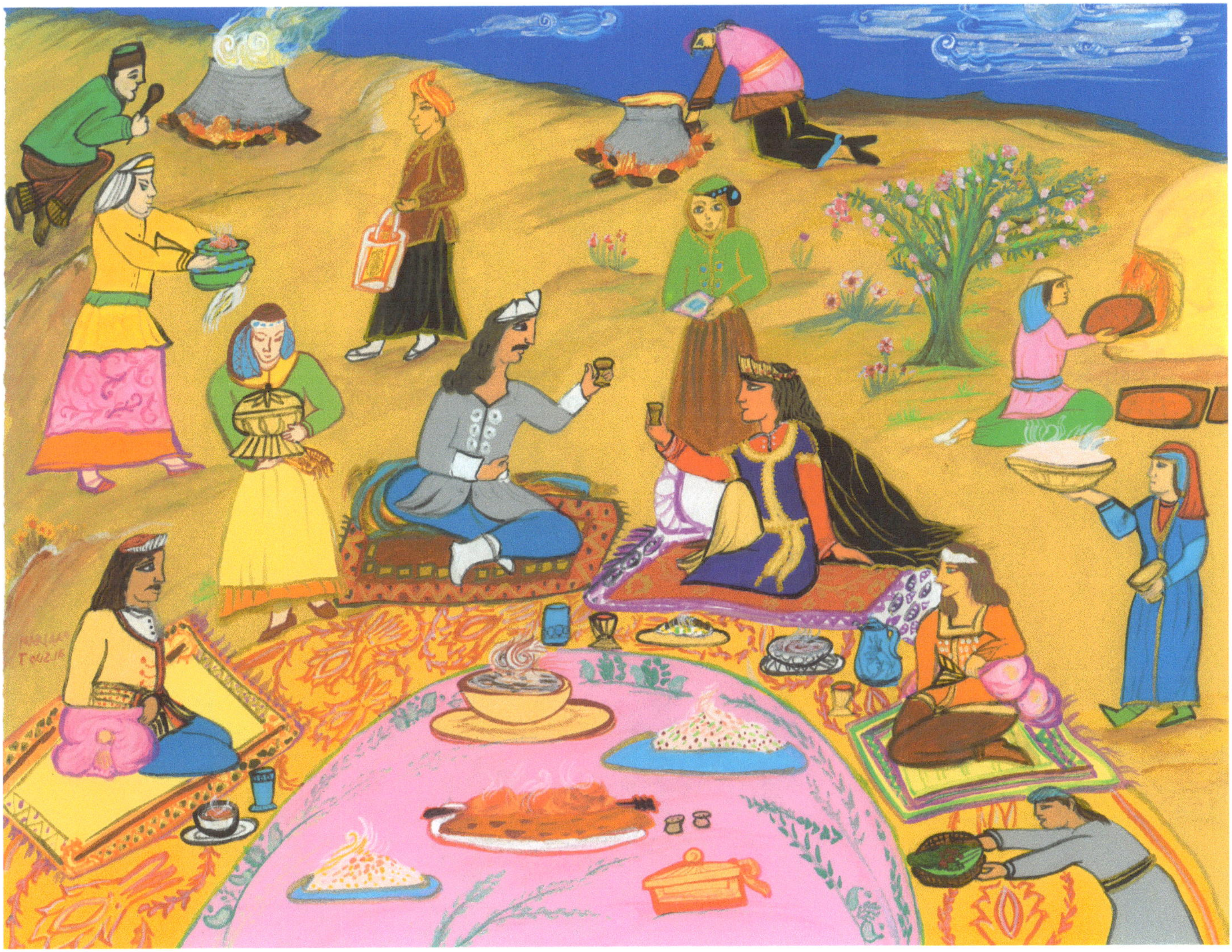

The King leaves the capital and comes all the way north just to welcome the warrior on his return. They meet at the beach town of Amol by the Caspian Sea.

The King and his most beloved warrior, Saum, settle state affairs harmoniously. But the love of Zal and Roudabeh sheds a dark light on the meeting, just as Mehrab had predicted! The King reminds Saum of the atrocities of Zahhak as told by the kings before him. "The child of such a marriage could endanger the whole country! It's unfathomable to me how Zahhak turned into a beast with the two snakes on his shoulders. And who knows what idols they worship now in Kabol…"

The King continues: "We owe so much to the bravery of Kaveh the Ironsmith who with his sons joined other fierce fighters to banish Zahhak after so many years." Then the king falls quiet. Saum is quiet too. He knows the king is unreceptive to any word of insight now. He offers none. He has none to offer. His hope has left him. The possibility of his son becoming the cause of atrocities y fades the last trace of hope in his heart. Now he can only think of the snakes on Zahhak's shoulders and their ravenous appetite for the brains of youth, the only food on which they fed.

"We must prevent such atrocities," the King announces. "Our strategy must be to exert force to keep people safe from another beast!" And he concludes: "Mehrab must know that this calls for a war!"

Saum has nothing to say. The truth is now obscured in his mind.

In Kabol, Saum and his loyal army meet Zal. Even without the sound of war drums, the reason for this arrival is apparent to Zal. He kisses the ground before his father and says: "Come, my brave father, and stay here in my camp, in the land of Roudabeh. Then you will know there is no evil here. You must trust me on that."

"I was raised in the wild and when I came with you to live among men I only asked to be allowed to live in peace," Zal reminds his father. Saum remembers his promise and resolves to ask his King that as a reward for his long years of battle protecting the land from demons the King should allow his son to live his life in peace.

Saum writes to the King, praising his governing of the country but asks him to relinquish his war plan. Zal takes the letter to the King and Saum returns to his mansion awaiting response in anticipation!

When Ceendokht reaches Zabolestan Saum is still anxiously waiting for the King's reply.

Sitting among his close friends informants tell Saum of the arrival of a lady messenger from Kabol! "A lady messenger with many peace offerings...!" whispers an informant in Saum's ears.

The warrior accepts the lady. She begins speaking immediately: "I am Ceendokht, queen of Kabol and mother of Roudabeh. I am here before you to say that you have done nothing wrong. If there is a fault, it is my husband's. Roudabeh is fair, full of charms and hopes. But above all, I am here for the people of Kabol," Ceendokht adds. "We are not idol worshipers! If you pray before the fire I won't call you a fire-worshipper. I know that idols are only symbols of our creator – the same creator as yours. There is no cause for war here." She utters her words with such conviction and passion that everyone in the room is spellbound.

Then she gets up and walks toward Saum only to say: "Please promise me peace."

"I do dear queen," Saum responds.

In the capital, King Manoochehr receives Zal with great joy. He reads the letter and asks Zal to stay with him. "I would like to have a feast in your honor," says the King.

Zal accepts with pleasure. The days of the feast are interwoven with many tests and debates for Zal. He raises awe both in the battlefield and in intellect.

Then one day King Manoochehr calls Zal to his quarters. "I am so glad to have you here all the time, but I believe you are aching to be with your father and the one whom you love in Kabol!" says the King with a bright smile on his face.

"Yes, my King."

"Then be on your way!"

Ceendohht is beside herself! She arranges the most beautiful and memorable wedding in anyone's memory.

The End

Mariam Touzie was born in Tehran, Iran. She graduated from Tehran University in Fine Arts. She then moved to New York City, continuing her studies at the School of Visual Arts where she received her masters degree and was awarded the Paula Rhodes prize for exquisite artwork.

Her series of illustrated books; "*Chronicles of Seemorgh & The Three Warriors*," consists of three books —"*Birth*," "*Love*," and "*Baby*."

To learn more of her art works please check: www.mariamtouzie.blogspot.com

ZAYANDEH PUBLICATIONS

www.ingramcontent.com/pod-product-compliance
Lightning Source LLC
Chambersburg PA
CBHW060808270326
41927CB00003B/86